Introduction

My parents gave me my first lock-style diary when I was in middle school. Back then, I mostly wrote about friendships, both happy and heartbreaking, and how much I loved my family and pets. As I got older, my diary shifted to school adventures, boy troubles, and dreams of one day moving to 'Hollywood'.

Throughout my life, journaling has remained a constant. It helped me track daily schedules, capture milestones, and reflect on the seasons of life. But it became an absolutely vital tool when I began caregiving. Suddenly, my journal wasn't just for memories; it became my roadmap. I used it to record my parents' schedules, appointments, and health issues.

Over time, my journal helped me recognize patterns and changes in their diseases, and gave me a better understand where they each were in their journeys with dementia. More importantly, it revealed how God was carrying me through each day and night, often in ways I didn't notice in the moment.

Over the years, I have received many beautiful journals as gifts, but most didn't quite fit my needs. Some were filled with too much unnecessary content; others didn't leave enough space to capture the important details of caregiving life.

I created this journal based on the following four categories I found myself needing every single day:

Today's Challenges: Use this section to organize your ever-changing schedule including doctor's appointments, calls to make, visits to plan, and basically anything essential for managing your challenging daily life.

A Moment of Grace: Even on the darkest days, something small will often shine through, a moment that makes you whisper, "Thank you, Jesus, I needed that." Maybe your loved one had a moment of clarity. Or perhaps a walk outside gave you a breath of peace. Use this space to record those glimpses of His grace.

What I Learned Today: Every caregiving day teaches something, sometimes hard lessons, sometimes beautiful ones. Writing them down helps you see the journey more clearly and reminds you in a month or a year just how far you've come with God's help.

Prayer for Strength: Caregiving is not for the faint of heart. Some days, surviving intact is only possible through prayer and grace. Use this space to write a prayer for strength, patience, understanding, or gratitude. Later, you'll have a testimony to share of how God carried you through each storm.

When you reach the end of your caregiving journey, these pages will be more than memories. They will be a testament of grace, strength, and God's steadfast presence through it all.

Much love to all of you and I'm saying a prayer to our Lord and Savior Jesus Christ right now for you and your family.

Ann-Marie Murrell

Date: _____

Scripture of the Day: _____

Today's Challenges:

_____
_____
_____
_____
_____

A Moment of Grace:

_____
_____
_____
_____
_____

What I'm Learning Through This Journey:

_____
_____
_____
_____

Prayer for Strength:

_____
_____
_____
_____

Date: _____

Scripture of the Day: _____

Today's Challenges:

_____
_____
_____
_____
_____

A Moment of Grace:

_____
_____
_____
_____
_____

What I'm Learning Through This Journey:

_____
_____
_____
_____
_____

Prayer for Strength:

_____
_____
_____
_____
_____

Date: _____

Scripture of the Day: _____

Today's Challenges:

_____
_____
_____
_____
_____

A Moment of Grace:

_____
_____
_____
_____
_____

What I'm Learning Through This Journey:

_____
_____
_____
_____
_____

Prayer for Strength:

_____
_____
_____
_____
_____

Date: _____

Scripture of the Day: _____

Today's Challenges:

_____
_____
_____
_____
_____

A Moment of Grace:

_____
_____
_____
_____
_____

What I'm Learning Through This Journey:

_____
_____
_____
_____
_____

Prayer for Strength:

_____
_____
_____
_____
_____

Date: _____

Scripture of the Day: _____

Today's Challenges:

_____
_____
_____
_____
_____

A Moment of Grace:

_____
_____
_____
_____
_____

What I'm Learning Through This Journey:

_____
_____
_____
_____
_____

Prayer for Strength:

_____
_____
_____
_____
_____

Date: _____

Scripture of the Day: _____

Today's Challenges:

_____
_____
_____
_____
_____

A Moment of Grace:

_____
_____
_____
_____

What I'm Learning Through This Journey:

_____
_____
_____
_____
_____

Prayer for Strength:

_____
_____
_____
_____

Date: _____

Scripture of the Day: _____

Today's Challenges:

_____
_____
_____
_____
_____

A Moment of Grace:

_____
_____
_____
_____
_____

What I'm Learning Through This Journey:

_____
_____
_____
_____

Prayer for Strength:

_____
_____
_____
_____
_____

Date: _____

Scripture of the Day: _____

Today's Challenges:

_____
_____
_____
_____
_____

A Moment of Grace:

_____
_____
_____
_____

What I'm Learning Through This Journey:

_____
_____
_____
_____

Prayer for Strength:

_____
_____
_____
_____

Date: _____

Scripture of the Day: _____

Today's Challenges:

_____

_____

_____

_____

_____

A Moment of Grace:

_____

_____

_____

_____

_____

What I'm Learning Through This Journey:

_____

_____

_____

_____

_____

Prayer for Strength:

_____

_____

_____

_____

Date: _____

Scripture of the Day: _____

Today's Challenges:

_____

_____

_____

_____

_____

A Moment of Grace:

_____

_____

_____

_____

_____

What I'm Learning Through This Journey:

_____

_____

_____

_____

_____

Prayer for Strength:

_____

_____

_____

_____

Date: _____

Scripture of the Day: _____

Today's Challenges:

_____
_____
_____
_____
_____

A Moment of Grace:

_____
_____
_____
_____
_____

What I'm Learning Through This Journey:

_____
_____
_____
_____
_____

Prayer for Strength:

_____
_____
_____
_____

Date: _____

Scripture of the Day: _____

Today's Challenges:

_____
_____
_____
_____
_____

A Moment of Grace:

_____
_____
_____
_____
_____

What I'm Learning Through This Journey:

_____
_____
_____
_____
_____

Prayer for Strength:

_____
_____
_____
_____
_____

Date: _____

Scripture of the Day: _____

Today's Challenges:

_____
_____
_____
_____
_____

A Moment of Grace:

_____
_____
_____
_____
_____

What I'm Learning Through This Journey:

_____
_____
_____
_____
_____

Prayer for Strength:

_____
_____
_____
_____
_____

Date: _____

Scripture of the Day: _____

Today's Challenges:

_____
_____
_____
_____
_____

A Moment of Grace:

_____
_____
_____
_____
_____

What I'm Learning Through This Journey:

_____
_____
_____
_____
_____

Prayer for Strength:

_____
_____
_____
_____
_____

Date: _____

Scripture of the Day: _____

Today's Challenges:

_____
_____
_____
_____
_____

A Moment of Grace:

_____
_____
_____
_____
_____

What I'm Learning Through This Journey:

_____
_____
_____
_____
_____

Prayer for Strength:

_____
_____
_____
_____
_____

Date: _____

Scripture of the Day: _____

Today's Challenges:

_____
_____
_____
_____
_____

A Moment of Grace:

_____
_____
_____
_____

What I'm Learning Through This Journey:

_____
_____
_____
_____

Prayer for Strength:

_____
_____
_____
_____

Date: _____

Scripture of the Day: _____

Today's Challenges:

_____
_____
_____
_____
_____

A Moment of Grace:

_____
_____
_____
_____
_____

What I'm Learning Through This Journey:

_____
_____
_____
_____
_____

Prayer for Strength:

_____
_____
_____
_____
_____

Date: _____

Scripture of the Day: _____

Today's Challenges:

_____

_____

_____

_____

_____

A Moment of Grace:

_____

_____

_____

_____

_____

What I'm Learning Through This Journey:

_____

_____

_____

_____

_____

Prayer for Strength:

_____

_____

_____

_____

_____

Date: _____

Scripture of the Day: _____

Today's Challenges:

_____
_____
_____
_____
_____

A Moment of Grace:

_____
_____
_____
_____
_____

What I'm Learning Through This Journey:

_____
_____
_____
_____
_____

Prayer for Strength:

_____
_____
_____
_____
_____

Date: _____

Scripture of the Day: _____

Today's Challenges:

_____
_____
_____
_____
_____

A Moment of Grace:

_____
_____
_____
_____
_____

What I'm Learning Through This Journey:

_____
_____
_____
_____
_____

Prayer for Strength:

_____
_____
_____
_____
_____

Date: _____

Scripture of the Day: _____

Today's Challenges:

_____
_____
_____
_____
_____

A Moment of Grace:

_____
_____
_____
_____
_____

What I'm Learning Through This Journey:

_____
_____
_____
_____
_____

Prayer for Strength:

_____
_____
_____
_____
_____

Date: _____

Scripture of the Day: _____

Today's Challenges:

_____
_____
_____
_____
_____

A Moment of Grace:

_____
_____
_____
_____
_____

What I'm Learning Through This Journey:

_____
_____
_____
_____
_____

Prayer for Strength:

_____
_____
_____
_____
_____

Date: _____

Scripture of the Day: _____

Today's Challenges:

_____
_____
_____
_____
_____

A Moment of Grace:

_____
_____
_____
_____
_____

What I'm Learning Through This Journey:

_____
_____
_____
_____
_____

Prayer for Strength:

_____
_____
_____
_____
_____

Date: _____

Scripture of the Day: _____

Today's Challenges:

_____
_____
_____
_____
_____

A Moment of Grace:

_____
_____
_____
_____
_____

What I'm Learning Through This Journey:

_____
_____
_____
_____
_____

Prayer for Strength:

_____
_____
_____
_____

Date: _____

Scripture of the Day: _____

Today's Challenges:

_____
_____
_____
_____
_____

A Moment of Grace:

_____
_____
_____
_____
_____

What I'm Learning Through This Journey:

_____
_____
_____
_____

Prayer for Strength:

_____
_____
_____
_____
_____

Date: _____

Scripture of the Day: _____

Today's Challenges:

_____
_____
_____
_____
_____

A Moment of Grace:

_____
_____
_____
_____
_____

What I'm Learning Through This Journey:

_____
_____
_____
_____
_____

Prayer for Strength:

_____
_____
_____
_____
_____

Date: _____

Scripture of the Day: _____

Today's Challenges:

_____
_____
_____
_____
_____

A Moment of Grace:

_____
_____
_____
_____
_____

What I'm Learning Through This Journey:

_____
_____
_____
_____
_____

Prayer for Strength:

_____
_____
_____
_____
_____

Date: _____

Scripture of the Day: _____

Today's Challenges:

_____
_____
_____
_____
_____

A Moment of Grace:

_____
_____
_____
_____
_____

What I'm Learning Through This Journey:

_____
_____
_____
_____
_____

Prayer for Strength:

_____
_____
_____
_____
_____

Date: _____

Scripture of the Day: _____

Today's Challenges:

_____
_____
_____
_____
_____

A Moment of Grace:

_____
_____
_____
_____
_____

What I'm Learning Through This Journey:

_____
_____
_____
_____
_____

Prayer for Strength:

_____
_____
_____
_____
_____

Date: _____

Scripture of the Day: _____

Today's Challenges:

_____
_____
_____
_____
_____

A Moment of Grace:

_____
_____
_____
_____

What I'm Learning Through This Journey:

_____
_____
_____
_____

Prayer for Strength:

_____
_____
_____
_____

Date: _____

Scripture of the Day: _____

Today's Challenges:

_____
_____
_____
_____
_____

A Moment of Grace:

_____
_____
_____
_____
_____

What I'm Learning Through This Journey:

_____
_____
_____
_____
_____

Prayer for Strength:

_____
_____
_____
_____
_____

Date: _____

Scripture of the Day: _____

Today's Challenges:

_____
_____
_____
_____
_____

A Moment of Grace:

_____
_____
_____
_____
_____

What I'm Learning Through This Journey:

_____
_____
_____
_____
_____

Prayer for Strength:

_____
_____
_____
_____
_____

Date: _____

Scripture of the Day: _____

Today's Challenges:

_____
_____
_____
_____
_____

A Moment of Grace:

_____
_____
_____
_____
_____

What I'm Learning Through This Journey:

_____
_____
_____
_____
_____

Prayer for Strength:

_____
_____
_____
_____
_____

Date: _____

Scripture of the Day: _____

Today's Challenges:

_____
_____
_____
_____
_____

A Moment of Grace:

_____
_____
_____
_____
_____

What I'm Learning Through This Journey:

_____
_____
_____
_____
_____

Prayer for Strength:

_____
_____
_____
_____
_____

Date: _____

Scripture of the Day: _____

Today's Challenges:

_____
_____
_____
_____
_____

A Moment of Grace:

_____
_____
_____
_____
_____

What I'm Learning Through This Journey:

_____
_____
_____
_____
_____

Prayer for Strength:

_____
_____
_____
_____
_____

Date: _____

Scripture of the Day: _____

Today's Challenges:

_____
_____
_____
_____
_____

A Moment of Grace:

_____
_____
_____
_____
_____

What I'm Learning Through This Journey:

_____
_____
_____
_____
_____

Prayer for Strength:

_____
_____
_____
_____
_____

Date: _____

Scripture of the Day: _____

Today's Challenges:

_____
_____
_____
_____
_____

A Moment of Grace:

_____
_____
_____
_____
_____

What I'm Learning Through This Journey:

_____
_____
_____
_____
_____

Prayer for Strength:

_____
_____
_____
_____
_____

Date: _____

Scripture of the Day: _____

Today's Challenges:

_____
_____
_____
_____
_____

A Moment of Grace:

_____
_____
_____
_____
_____

What I'm Learning Through This Journey:

_____
_____
_____
_____
_____

Prayer for Strength:

_____
_____
_____
_____
_____

Date: _____

Scripture of the Day: _____

Today's Challenges:

_____
_____
_____
_____
_____

A Moment of Grace:

_____
_____
_____
_____
_____

What I'm Learning Through This Journey:

_____
_____
_____
_____
_____

Prayer for Strength:

_____
_____
_____
_____
_____

Date: _____

Scripture of the Day: _____

Today's Challenges:

_____
_____
_____
_____
_____

A Moment of Grace:

_____
_____
_____
_____
_____

What I'm Learning Through This Journey:

_____
_____
_____
_____
_____

Prayer for Strength:

_____
_____
_____
_____
_____

Date: _____

Scripture of the Day: _____

Today's Challenges:

_____
_____
_____
_____
_____

A Moment of Grace:

_____
_____
_____
_____

What I'm Learning Through This Journey:

_____
_____
_____
_____

Prayer for Strength:

_____
_____
_____
_____

Date: _____

Scripture of the Day: _____

Today's Challenges:

_____
_____
_____
_____
_____

A Moment of Grace:

_____
_____
_____
_____
_____

What I'm Learning Through This Journey:

_____
_____
_____
_____
_____

Prayer for Strength:

_____
_____
_____
_____
_____

Date: _____

Scripture of the Day: _____

Today's Challenges:

_____
_____
_____
_____
_____

A Moment of Grace:

_____
_____
_____
_____
_____

What I'm Learning Through This Journey:

_____
_____
_____
_____
_____

Prayer for Strength:

_____
_____
_____
_____
_____

Date: _____

Scripture of the Day: _____

Today's Challenges:

_____
_____
_____
_____
_____

A Moment of Grace:

_____
_____
_____
_____
_____

What I'm Learning Through This Journey:

_____
_____
_____
_____
_____

Prayer for Strength:

_____
_____
_____
_____
_____

Date: _____

Scripture of the Day: _____

Today's Challenges:

_____

_____

_____

_____

_____

A Moment of Grace:

_____

_____

_____

_____

_____

What I'm Learning Through This Journey:

_____

_____

_____

_____

_____

Prayer for Strength:

_____

_____

_____

_____

_____

Date: _____

Scripture of the Day: _____

Today's Challenges:

_____
_____
_____
_____
_____

A Moment of Grace:

_____
_____
_____
_____
_____

What I'm Learning Through This Journey:

_____
_____
_____
_____
_____

Prayer for Strength:

_____
_____
_____
_____
_____

Date: _____

Scripture of the Day: _____

Today's Challenges:

_____
_____
_____
_____
_____

A Moment of Grace:

_____
_____
_____
_____
_____

What I'm Learning Through This Journey:

_____
_____
_____
_____
_____

Prayer for Strength:

_____
_____
_____
_____

Date: _____

Scripture of the Day: _____

Today's Challenges:

_____
_____
_____
_____
_____

A Moment of Grace:

_____
_____
_____
_____
_____

What I'm Learning Through This Journey:

_____
_____
_____
_____
_____

Prayer for Strength:

_____
_____
_____
_____
_____

Date: _____

Scripture of the Day: _____

Today's Challenges:

_____

_____

_____

_____

_____

A Moment of Grace:

_____

_____

_____

_____

_____

What I'm Learning Through This Journey:

_____

_____

_____

_____

_____

Prayer for Strength:

_____

_____

_____

_____

Date: _____

Scripture of the Day: _____

Today's Challenges:

_____
_____
_____
_____
_____

A Moment of Grace:

_____
_____
_____
_____

What I'm Learning Through This Journey:

_____
_____
_____
_____

Prayer for Strength:

_____
_____
_____
_____

Date: _____

Scripture of the Day: _____

Today's Challenges:

_____
_____
_____
_____
_____

A Moment of Grace:

_____
_____
_____
_____
_____

What I'm Learning Through This Journey:

_____
_____
_____
_____
_____

Prayer for Strength:

_____
_____
_____
_____

Date: _____

Scripture of the Day: _____

Today's Challenges:

_____
_____
_____
_____
_____

A Moment of Grace:

_____
_____
_____
_____
_____

What I'm Learning Through This Journey:

_____
_____
_____
_____
_____

Prayer for Strength:

_____
_____
_____
_____
_____

Date: _____

Scripture of the Day: _____

Today's Challenges:

_____
_____
_____
_____
_____

A Moment of Grace:

_____
_____
_____
_____
_____

What I'm Learning Through This Journey:

_____
_____
_____
_____
_____

Prayer for Strength:

_____
_____
_____
_____
_____

Date: _____

Scripture of the Day: _____

Today's Challenges:

_____

_____

_____

_____

_____

A Moment of Grace:

_____

_____

_____

_____

What I'm Learning Through This Journey:

_____

_____

_____

_____

Prayer for Strength:

_____

_____

_____

_____

Date: _____

Scripture of the Day: _____

Today's Challenges:

_____
_____
_____
_____
_____

A Moment of Grace:

_____
_____
_____
_____

What I'm Learning Through This Journey:

_____
_____
_____
_____

Prayer for Strength:

_____
_____
_____
_____

Date: _____

Scripture of the Day: _____

Today's Challenges:

_____

_____

_____

_____

_____

A Moment of Grace:

_____

_____

_____

_____

_____

What I'm Learning Through This Journey:

_____

_____

_____

_____

_____

Prayer for Strength:

_____

_____

_____

_____

_____

Date: _____

Scripture of the Day: _____

Today's Challenges:

_____
_____
_____
_____
_____

A Moment of Grace:

_____
_____
_____
_____
_____

What I'm Learning Through This Journey:

_____
_____
_____
_____
_____

Prayer for Strength:

_____
_____
_____
_____
_____

Date: _____

Scripture of the Day: _____

Today's Challenges:

_____
_____
_____
_____
_____

A Moment of Grace:

_____
_____
_____
_____
_____

What I'm Learning Through This Journey:

_____
_____
_____
_____
_____

Prayer for Strength:

_____
_____
_____
_____
_____

Date: _____

Scripture of the Day: _____

Today's Challenges:

_____
_____
_____
_____
_____

A Moment of Grace:

_____
_____
_____
_____
_____

What I'm Learning Through This Journey:

_____
_____
_____
_____
_____

Prayer for Strength:

_____
_____
_____
_____
_____

Date: _____

Scripture of the Day: _____

Today's Challenges:

_____

_____

_____

_____

_____

A Moment of Grace:

_____

_____

_____

_____

What I'm Learning Through This Journey:

_____

_____

_____

_____

Prayer for Strength:

_____

_____

_____

_____

Date: _____

Scripture of the Day: _____

Today's Challenges:

_____
_____
_____
_____
_____

A Moment of Grace:

_____
_____
_____
_____
_____

What I'm Learning Through This Journey:

_____
_____
_____
_____
_____

Prayer for Strength:

_____
_____
_____
_____
_____

Date: _____

Scripture of the Day: _____

Today's Challenges:

_____
_____
_____
_____
_____

A Moment of Grace:

_____
_____
_____
_____
_____

What I'm Learning Through This Journey:

_____
_____
_____
_____
_____

Prayer for Strength:

_____
_____
_____
_____
_____

Date: _____

Scripture of the Day: _____

Today's Challenges:

_____

_____

_____

_____

_____

A Moment of Grace:

_____

_____

_____

_____

_____

What I'm Learning Through This Journey:

_____

_____

_____

_____

_____

Prayer for Strength:

_____

_____

_____

_____

_____

Date: _____

Scripture of the Day: _____

Today's Challenges:

_____
_____
_____
_____
_____

A Moment of Grace:

_____
_____
_____
_____
_____

What I'm Learning Through This Journey:

_____
_____
_____
_____
_____

Prayer for Strength:

_____
_____
_____
_____
_____

Date: _____

Scripture of the Day: _____

Today's Challenges:

_____
_____
_____
_____
_____

A Moment of Grace:

_____
_____
_____
_____
_____

What I'm Learning Through This Journey:

_____
_____
_____
_____

Prayer for Strength:

_____
_____
_____
_____
_____

Date: _____

Scripture of the Day: _____

Today's Challenges:

_____
_____
_____
_____
_____

A Moment of Grace:

_____
_____
_____
_____
_____

What I'm Learning Through This Journey:

_____
_____
_____
_____
_____

Prayer for Strength:

_____
_____
_____
_____
_____

Date: _____

Scripture of the Day: _____

Today's Challenges:

_____
_____
_____
_____
_____

A Moment of Grace:

_____
_____
_____
_____
_____

What I'm Learning Through This Journey:

_____
_____
_____
_____

Prayer for Strength:

_____
_____
_____
_____
_____

Date: _____

Scripture of the Day: _____

Today's Challenges:

_____
_____
_____
_____
_____

A Moment of Grace:

_____
_____
_____
_____
_____

What I'm Learning Through This Journey:

_____
_____
_____
_____
_____

Prayer for Strength:

_____
_____
_____
_____
_____

Date: _____

Scripture of the Day: _____

Today's Challenges:

_____
_____
_____
_____
_____

A Moment of Grace:

_____
_____
_____
_____
_____

What I'm Learning Through This Journey:

_____
_____
_____
_____
_____

Prayer for Strength:

_____
_____
_____
_____
_____

Date: _____

Scripture of the Day: _____

Today's Challenges:

_____
_____
_____
_____
_____

A Moment of Grace:

_____
_____
_____
_____
_____

What I'm Learning Through This Journey:

_____
_____
_____
_____
_____

Prayer for Strength:

_____
_____
_____
_____
_____

Date: _____

Scripture of the Day: _____

Today's Challenges:

_____
_____
_____
_____
_____

A Moment of Grace:

_____
_____
_____
_____
_____

What I'm Learning Through This Journey:

_____
_____
_____
_____

Prayer for Strength:

_____
_____
_____
_____

Date: _____

Scripture of the Day: _____

Today's Challenges:

_____
_____
_____
_____
_____

A Moment of Grace:

_____
_____
_____
_____
_____

What I'm Learning Through This Journey:

_____
_____
_____
_____
_____

Prayer for Strength:

_____
_____
_____
_____

Date: _____

Scripture of the Day: _____

Today's Challenges:

_____
_____
_____
_____
_____

A Moment of Grace:

_____
_____
_____
_____

What I'm Learning Through This Journey:

_____
_____
_____
_____

Prayer for Strength:

_____
_____
_____
_____

Date: _____

Scripture of the Day: _____

Today's Challenges:

_____
_____
_____
_____
_____

A Moment of Grace:

_____
_____
_____
_____
_____

What I'm Learning Through This Journey:

_____
_____
_____
_____
_____

Prayer for Strength:

_____
_____
_____
_____
_____

Date: _____

Scripture of the Day: _____

Today's Challenges:

_____
_____
_____
_____
_____

A Moment of Grace:

_____
_____
_____
_____
_____

What I'm Learning Through This Journey:

_____
_____
_____
_____
_____

Prayer for Strength:

_____
_____
_____
_____
_____

Date: _____

Scripture of the Day: _____

Today's Challenges:

_____
_____
_____
_____
_____

A Moment of Grace:

_____
_____
_____
_____
_____

What I'm Learning Through This Journey:

_____
_____
_____
_____

Prayer for Strength:

_____
_____
_____
_____

Date: _____

Scripture of the Day: _____

Today's Challenges:

_____
_____
_____
_____
_____

A Moment of Grace:

_____
_____
_____
_____
_____

What I'm Learning Through This Journey:

_____
_____
_____
_____
_____

Prayer for Strength:

_____
_____
_____
_____
_____

Date: _____

Scripture of the Day: _____

Today's Challenges:

_____
_____
_____
_____
_____

A Moment of Grace:

_____
_____
_____
_____

What I'm Learning Through This Journey:

_____
_____
_____
_____

Prayer for Strength:

_____
_____
_____
_____

Date: _____

Scripture of the Day: _____

Today's Challenges:

_____
_____
_____
_____
_____

A Moment of Grace:

_____
_____
_____
_____
_____

What I'm Learning Through This Journey:

_____
_____
_____
_____
_____

Prayer for Strength:

_____
_____
_____
_____

Date: _____

Scripture of the Day: _____

Today's Challenges:

_____

_____

_____

_____

_____

A Moment of Grace:

_____

_____

_____

_____

_____

What I'm Learning Through This Journey:

_____

_____

_____

_____

_____

Prayer for Strength:

_____

_____

_____

_____

Date: _____

Scripture of the Day: _____

Today's Challenges:

_____
_____
_____
_____
_____

A Moment of Grace:

_____
_____
_____
_____
_____

What I'm Learning Through This Journey:

_____
_____
_____
_____
_____

Prayer for Strength:

_____
_____
_____
_____

Date: _____

Scripture of the Day: _____

Today's Challenges:

_____
_____
_____
_____
_____

A Moment of Grace:

_____
_____
_____
_____
_____

What I'm Learning Through This Journey:

_____
_____
_____
_____
_____

Prayer for Strength:

_____
_____
_____
_____
_____

Date: _____

Scripture of the Day: _____

Today's Challenges:

_____
_____
_____
_____
_____

A Moment of Grace:

_____
_____
_____
_____
_____

What I'm Learning Through This Journey:

_____
_____
_____
_____
_____

Prayer for Strength:

_____
_____
_____
_____

Date: _____

Scripture of the Day: _____

Today's Challenges:

_____
_____
_____
_____
_____

A Moment of Grace:

_____
_____
_____
_____
_____

What I'm Learning Through This Journey:

_____
_____
_____
_____
_____

Prayer for Strength:

_____
_____
_____
_____
_____

Date: _____

Scripture of the Day: _____

Today's Challenges:

_____
_____
_____
_____
_____

A Moment of Grace:

_____
_____
_____
_____
_____

What I'm Learning Through This Journey:

_____
_____
_____
_____
_____

Prayer for Strength:

_____
_____
_____
_____
_____

Date: _____

Scripture of the Day: _____

Today's Challenges:

_____
_____
_____
_____
_____

A Moment of Grace:

_____
_____
_____
_____
_____

What I'm Learning Through This Journey:

_____
_____
_____
_____
_____

Prayer for Strength:

_____
_____
_____
_____
_____

Date: _____

Scripture of the Day: _____

Today's Challenges:

_____
_____
_____
_____
_____

A Moment of Grace:

_____
_____
_____
_____
_____

What I'm Learning Through This Journey:

_____
_____
_____
_____
_____

Prayer for Strength:

_____
_____
_____
_____

Date: _____

Scripture of the Day: _____

Today's Challenges:

_____
_____
_____
_____
_____

A Moment of Grace:

_____
_____
_____
_____
_____

What I'm Learning Through This Journey:

_____
_____
_____
_____
_____

Prayer for Strength:

_____
_____
_____
_____
_____

Date: _____

Scripture of the Day: _____

Today's Challenges:

_____
_____
_____
_____
_____

A Moment of Grace:

_____
_____
_____
_____
_____

What I'm Learning Through This Journey:

_____
_____
_____
_____
_____

Prayer for Strength:

_____
_____
_____
_____

Date: _____

Scripture of the Day: _____

Today's Challenges:

_____
_____
_____
_____
_____

A Moment of Grace:

_____
_____
_____
_____
_____

What I'm Learning Through This Journey:

_____
_____
_____
_____
_____

Prayer for Strength:

_____
_____
_____
_____
_____

Date: _____

Scripture of the Day: _____

Today's Challenges:

_____
_____
_____
_____
_____

A Moment of Grace:

_____
_____
_____
_____
_____

What I'm Learning Through This Journey:

_____
_____
_____
_____
_____

Prayer for Strength:

_____
_____
_____
_____
_____

Date: _____

Scripture of the Day: _____

Today's Challenges:

_____
_____
_____
_____
_____

A Moment of Grace:

_____
_____
_____
_____
_____

What I'm Learning Through This Journey:

_____
_____
_____
_____
_____

Prayer for Strength:

_____
_____
_____
_____

Date: _____

Scripture of the Day: _____

Today's Challenges:

_____
_____
_____
_____
_____

A Moment of Grace:

_____
_____
_____
_____
_____

What I'm Learning Through This Journey:

_____
_____
_____
_____
_____

Prayer for Strength:

_____
_____
_____
_____

Date: _____

Scripture of the Day: _____

Today's Challenges:

_____
_____
_____
_____
_____

A Moment of Grace:

_____
_____
_____
_____
_____

What I'm Learning Through This Journey:

_____
_____
_____
_____
_____

Prayer for Strength:

_____
_____
_____
_____
_____

Date: _____

Scripture of the Day: _____

Today's Challenges:

_____
_____
_____
_____
_____

A Moment of Grace:

_____
_____
_____
_____
_____

What I'm Learning Through This Journey:

_____
_____
_____
_____
_____

Prayer for Strength:

_____
_____
_____
_____
_____

Date: _____

Scripture of the Day: _____

Today's Challenges:

_____
_____
_____
_____
_____

A Moment of Grace:

_____
_____
_____
_____
_____

What I'm Learning Through This Journey:

_____
_____
_____
_____
_____

Prayer for Strength:

_____
_____
_____
_____
_____

Date: _____

Scripture of the Day: _____

Today's Challenges:

_____
_____
_____
_____
_____

A Moment of Grace:

_____
_____
_____
_____
_____

What I'm Learning Through This Journey:

_____
_____
_____
_____
_____

Prayer for Strength:

_____
_____
_____
_____
_____

Date: _____

Scripture of the Day: _____

Today's Challenges:

_____
_____
_____
_____
_____

A Moment of Grace:

_____
_____
_____
_____
_____

What I'm Learning Through This Journey:

_____
_____
_____
_____
_____

Prayer for Strength:

_____
_____
_____
_____
_____

Date: _____

Scripture of the Day: _____

Today's Challenges:

_____
_____
_____
_____
_____

A Moment of Grace:

_____
_____
_____
_____
_____

What I'm Learning Through This Journey:

_____
_____
_____
_____
_____

Prayer for Strength:

_____
_____
_____
_____
_____

Date: _____

Scripture of the Day: _____

Today's Challenges:

_____
_____
_____
_____
_____

A Moment of Grace:

_____
_____
_____
_____
_____

What I'm Learning Through This Journey:

_____
_____
_____
_____
_____

Prayer for Strength:

_____
_____
_____
_____
_____

Date: _____

Scripture of the Day: _____

Today's Challenges:

_____
_____
_____
_____
_____

A Moment of Grace:

_____
_____
_____
_____
_____

What I'm Learning Through This Journey:

_____
_____
_____
_____

Prayer for Strength:

_____
_____
_____
_____

Date: _____

Scripture of the Day: _____

Today's Challenges:

_____
_____
_____
_____
_____

A Moment of Grace:

_____
_____
_____
_____
_____

What I'm Learning Through This Journey:

_____
_____
_____
_____
_____

Prayer for Strength:

_____
_____
_____
_____
_____

Date: _____

Scripture of the Day: _____

Today's Challenges:

_____
_____
_____
_____
_____

A Moment of Grace:

_____
_____
_____
_____
_____

What I'm Learning Through This Journey:

_____
_____
_____
_____
_____

Prayer for Strength:

_____
_____
_____
_____
_____

Date: _____

Scripture of the Day: _____

Today's Challenges:

_____
_____
_____
_____
_____

A Moment of Grace:

_____
_____
_____
_____
_____

What I'm Learning Through This Journey:

_____
_____
_____
_____
_____

Prayer for Strength:

_____
_____
_____
_____
_____

Date: _____

Scripture of the Day: _____

Today's Challenges:

_____
_____
_____
_____
_____

A Moment of Grace:

_____
_____
_____
_____
_____

What I'm Learning Through This Journey:

_____
_____
_____
_____
_____

Prayer for Strength:

_____
_____
_____
_____
_____

Date: _____

Scripture of the Day: _____

Today's Challenges:

_____
_____
_____
_____
_____

A Moment of Grace:

_____
_____
_____
_____
_____

What I'm Learning Through This Journey:

_____
_____
_____
_____

Prayer for Strength:

_____
_____
_____
_____
_____

Date: _____

Scripture of the Day: _____

Today's Challenges:

_____
_____
_____
_____
_____

A Moment of Grace:

_____
_____
_____
_____
_____

What I'm Learning Through This Journey:

_____
_____
_____
_____
_____

Prayer for Strength:

_____
_____
_____
_____
_____

Date: _____

Scripture of the Day: _____

Today's Challenges:

_____
_____
_____
_____
_____

A Moment of Grace:

_____
_____
_____
_____
_____

What I'm Learning Through This Journey:

_____
_____
_____
_____
_____

Prayer for Strength:

_____
_____
_____
_____
_____

Date: _____

Scripture of the Day: _____

Today's Challenges:

_____
_____
_____
_____
_____

A Moment of Grace:

_____
_____
_____
_____
_____

What I'm Learning Through This Journey:

_____
_____
_____
_____

Prayer for Strength:

_____
_____
_____
_____

Date: _____

Scripture of the Day: _____

Today's Challenges:

_____
_____
_____
_____
_____

A Moment of Grace:

_____
_____
_____
_____
_____

What I'm Learning Through This Journey:

_____
_____
_____
_____
_____

Prayer for Strength:

_____
_____
_____
_____
_____

Date: _____

Scripture of the Day: _____

Today's Challenges:

_____
_____
_____
_____
_____

A Moment of Grace:

_____
_____
_____
_____
_____

What I'm Learning Through This Journey:

_____
_____
_____
_____
_____

Prayer for Strength:

_____
_____
_____
_____

Date: _____

Scripture of the Day: _____

Today's Challenges:

_____
_____
_____
_____
_____

A Moment of Grace:

_____
_____
_____
_____
_____

What I'm Learning Through This Journey:

_____
_____
_____
_____

Prayer for Strength:

_____
_____
_____
_____

Date: _____

Scripture of the Day: _____

Today's Challenges:

_____
_____
_____
_____
_____

A Moment of Grace:

_____
_____
_____
_____
_____

What I'm Learning Through This Journey:

_____
_____
_____
_____
_____

Prayer for Strength:

_____
_____
_____
_____
_____

Date: _____

Scripture of the Day: _____

Today's Challenges:

_____
_____
_____
_____
_____

A Moment of Grace:

_____
_____
_____
_____
_____

What I'm Learning Through This Journey:

_____
_____
_____
_____
_____

Prayer for Strength:

_____
_____
_____
_____
_____

Date: _____

Scripture of the Day: _____

Today's Challenges:

_____
_____
_____
_____
_____

A Moment of Grace:

_____
_____
_____
_____
_____

What I'm Learning Through This Journey:

_____
_____
_____
_____
_____

Prayer for Strength:

_____
_____
_____
_____
_____

Date: _____

Scripture of the Day: _____

Today's Challenges:

_____

_____

_____

_____

_____

A Moment of Grace:

_____

_____

_____

_____

_____

What I'm Learning Through This Journey:

_____

_____

_____

_____

_____

Prayer for Strength:

_____

_____

_____

_____

_____

Date: _____

Scripture of the Day: _____

Today's Challenges:

_____
_____
_____
_____
_____

A Moment of Grace:

_____
_____
_____
_____
_____

What I'm Learning Through This Journey:

_____
_____
_____
_____
_____

Prayer for Strength:

_____
_____
_____
_____
_____

Date: _____

Scripture of the Day: _____

Today's Challenges:

_____
_____
_____
_____
_____

A Moment of Grace:

_____
_____
_____
_____
_____

What I'm Learning Through This Journey:

_____
_____
_____
_____
_____

Prayer for Strength:

_____
_____
_____
_____
_____

Date: _____

Scripture of the Day: _____

Today's Challenges:

_____
_____
_____
_____
_____

A Moment of Grace:

_____
_____
_____
_____

What I'm Learning Through This Journey:

_____
_____
_____
_____

Prayer for Strength:

_____
_____
_____
_____

Date: _____

Scripture of the Day: _____

Today's Challenges:

_____

_____

_____

_____

_____

A Moment of Grace:

_____

_____

_____

_____

_____

What I'm Learning Through This Journey:

_____

_____

_____

_____

_____

Prayer for Strength:

_____

_____

_____

_____

_____

www.ingramcontent.com/pod-product-compliance
Lightning Source LLC
Chambersburg PA
CBHW071322130626
46556CB00004B/1708